The New Business Kit

A Guide to Financial, Tax and Accounting Considerations of Successfully Starting a New Business

KLEIN HALL CPAs

Klein Hall CPAs, LLC

3957 75th Street

Aurora, IL 60504

(Located off 75th Street and Route 59)

T: 630.898.5578

F: 630.225.5128

KleinHallcpa.com

INTRODUCTION

Congratulations on your new business —
We wish you every success!

We have written this <u>New Business Kit</u> to provide you with basic information about the financial, tax and accounting considerations of starting a new business.

Many new businesses fail in the early years from poor management and lack of attention to financial basics such as record-keeping and reporting. That's where we come in — we want to be part of your team to make sure you have in place the things that will allow you to enjoy ongoing success.

Having a team of outside advisors is important — including a CPA, lawyer, bank manager and insurance agent — And make sure your advisors are willing to be <u>engaged</u> and <u>proactive</u> in helping you. You don't need spectators — you need coaches!

Klein Hall CPAs has been active in the Naperville Area since 1998. We specialize in four areas:

1.   Helping individuals and families with tax compliance and tax planning.

2.   Helping owner-managed businesses with their accounting, tax and consulting needs so that they can focus on running their businesses.

3.   Helping individuals and families with <u>comprehensive</u>, <u>holistic</u> wealth management, so that they can achieve financial independence and meet their life objectives.

4.   Helping expatriate individuals and families with their tax issues. This may involve Americans living abroad or more often citizens of other countries living in the United States, either permanently or temporarily on various types of visas. This is a complex area and requires careful planning and compliance.

Klein Hall CPAs | 630.898.5578 | KleinHallcpa.com

We would appreciate the opportunity to meet with you either at our office or yours — we are pleased to offer a one-hour complimentary consultation meeting.

Sincerely,

Klein Hall CPAs

PLEASE NOTE: While every effort has been made to provide the most up-to-date information, legislation does change. Please contact Klein Hall CPAs for the latest rates and IRS legislative updates.

TABLE OF CONTENTS

SELECTING A LEGAL ENTITY   **6**
    1. SOLE PROPRIETORSHIP..7
    2. PARTNERSHIP..8
    3. C CORPORATION..9
    4. S CORPORATION 10
    5. LIMITED LIABILITY COMPANY (LLC)....................................10
    6. FISCAL YEAR-END...11
REGISTERING WITH THE TAX AUTHORITIES   **13**
    1. INTERNAL REVENUE SERVICE..14
    2. ILLINOIS DEPARTMENT OF EMPLOYMENT SECURITY 15
    3. ILLINOIS DEPARTMENT OF REVENUE.................................15
    4. BUSINESS LICENSE..16
    5. TAX CALENDAR..16
FEDERAL AND STATE PAYROLL TAXES   **19**
    1. FEDERAL PAYROLL TAXES 20
    2. FEDERAL PAYROLL TAX DEPOSIT REQUIREMENTS 21
    3. FEDERAL UNEMPLOYMENT TAXES 22
    4. SUPPLEMENTAL WAGES 23
    5. FRINGE BENEFITS 23
    6. OTHER TAX REQUIREMENTS 24
    7. AVAILABLE PUBLICATIONS..25
    8. ILLINOIS PAYROLL TAXES 26
    9. ILLINOIS PAYROLL TAX DEPOSIT REQUIREMENTS 26
    10. EMPLOYEE VS. INDEPENDENT CONTRACTOR......................27
    11. ILLINOIS INDEPENDENT CONTRACTOR 32
    12. 1099 FILING REQUIREMENTS FOR INDEPENDENT CONTRACTORS 33
INCOME TAXES   **34**
    1. INCOME TAX REPORTING 35
    2. ESTIMATED TAX PAYMENTS 36
    3. DUE DATES 37
    4. EXTENSIONS..38
    5. FIRST TAX RETURN 38
    6. STATE TAXES 39
ACCOUNTING AND BOOKKEEPING   **40**
    1. THE ACCOUNTING PROCESS 42
    2. FINANCIAL STATEMENTS...43
    3. RESPONSIBILITY FOR BOOKKEEPING AND ACCOUNTING.......45
    4. CASH OR ACCRUAL ACCOUNTING...47
    5. INTERNAL CONTROL...47
    6. COMPUTER SYSTEMS...50

CASH MANAGEMENT   **51**
    1. STARTING THE ANALYSIS 52
    2. CASH COLLECTIONS 52
    3. CASH OUTFLOWS 53
FINANCING YOUR BUSINESS   **56**
    1. FINANCING ALTERNATIVES 58
    2. DEBT FINANCING SOURCES 58
    3. EQUITY FINANCING SOURCES...60
    4. HOW DO I GET THE MONEY?...61
INSURANCE   **63**
    1. POLICIES..64
SELECTING PROFESSIONAL ADVISORS   **68**
FEDERAL FORMS   **70**
ILLINOIS FORMS   **71**

CHAPTER 1

SELECTING A LEGAL ENTITY

*"Creating value for customers builds
loyalty, and loyalty in turn builds growth,
profit, and more value."*
Frederik Reichheld
The Loyalty Effect

CHAPTER 1

SELECTING A LEGAL ENTITY

Congratulations on being in business! One of the first things you will need to decide is what kind of legal entity you are going to use to conduct your activities. The decision depends on:

- How you intend to finance your business,
- The amount of personal risk you are willing to bear,
- Taxation,
- Who else is involved, and
- Any legal restrictions.

There are a number of options which are discussed below. This decision will have a significant impact on the way you are protected under the law, and the way you are affected by income tax rules and regulations. Each type of legal entity has its benefits and drawbacks, and each is treated differently for legal and tax purposes.

There are five basic forms of business organizations:

1.   SOLE PROPRIETORSHIP

A sole proprietorship is a business owned and operated by an individual or a married couple. It is not considered to be a legal entity in its own right, but rather an extension of the individual or individuals who own it. The business owner owns the business assets personally and is responsible for the debts or other liabilities of the business. The income or loss from a sole proprietorship is combined with the other earnings of an individual (or married couple) for income tax purposes.

A sole proprietorship is the simplest form of business to own and operate because it does not require any specific legal organization. It just needs to obtain any required licenses or permits.

2.   PARTNERSHIP

Partnerships can be structured as general partnerships or limited partnerships.

> **Successful Business Owners**
>
> 1. Know what the business will look like in 5 years
> 2. Have personal objectives in line with the business strategy
> 3. Know their exit plan
> 4. Work ON their business, and not just IN it

A **general partnership** is comprised of two or more individuals who go into business together. It will usually file a fictitious business name statement to operate under the partnership name. Each of the individual partners owns the company assets, has responsibility for its liabilities, and has authority to run the business. The authority of the partners and the way in which profits and losses are shared can be established by partnership agreement. Responsibility for liabilities can also be documented in an agreement, but partnership creditors typically have recourse to all the personal assets of each of the partners for settlement of partnership debts.

A **limited partnership** is comprised of one or more general partners and one or more limited partners. Limited partners do not take part in running the business and are not liable for the debts of the partnership. However, if a limited partner does take part in running the business, they become personally liable. All the general partners are personally liable.

The rights, responsibilities and obligations of both the limited and general partners are typically detailed in a partnership agreement. Whether you have a limited or general partnership, it is important to have a signed agreement.

A partnership is recognized under the law as a legal entity, and as such, has rights and responsibilities in and of itself. A partnership can enter into contracts, obtain trade credit and borrow money. Most creditors will require personal guarantees from the general partners when dealing with a small partnership.

A partnership is required to file both Federal and State Income Tax returns. However, a partnership does not generally pay income tax. Partnership income or loss is allocated to the individual partners and the partners report their shares of the net income or loss on their personal income tax returns.

3.   C CORPORATION

Corporations are regulated by state law which permits them to function as separate legal entities. A corporation has legal rights and is responsible for the corporation debts and filing income tax returns and paying taxes. Typically, owners or shareholders of a corporation are protected from the liabilities of the business. However, when a corporation is small, creditors may require personal guarantees from the principal owners before extending credit.

The first step is to prepare **Articles of Incorporation** and **By-laws** which are then adopted and filed; these govern the rights and obligations of the shareholders, directors and officers.

Corporations must file annual income tax returns with the IRS and their state's tax agency as well as other states where they do business. The elections made in a corporation's initial tax returns can have a significant impact on how the business is taxed in the future. Regular corporations (i.e. those that have not elected S status — see below) are referred to as C Corporations.

It is advisable to seek the assistance of an experienced lawyer and CPA when incorporating your business as there are a number of critical decisions to be made which will have far-reaching and long-lasting impact.

4. S CORPORATION

An S Corporation is treated like a regular corporation with one exception — an S Corporation pays no income tax. The net income or loss from the S Corporation is combined with the other income of the stockholders on their personal tax returns. There are special rules governing the deductibility of S Corporation losses, which are generally limited to an individual's tax basis. The tax laws regarding tax basis are quite complex.

S Corporation status is attained by filing Form 2553 which must be done in a timely manner. The decision as to whether to elect S status requires appropriate consultation prior to incorporation for new businesses or before filing the election for existing corporations. There are regulations regarding which corporations are eligible to be taxed as S Corporations. If a corporation was previously taxed as a C Corporation, there are additional tax considerations that may subject the S Corporation to a tax liability.

5. LIMITED LIABILITY COMPANY (LLC)

A Limited Liability Corporation (LLC) combines the liability protection of a corporation with the favorable tax treatment of a partnership. If an LLC has 2 or more members, it can elect to be treated as either a corporation or a partnership for income tax purposes and then files the appropriate tax forms. A single member LLC can disregard the entity and treat itself as though it were a sole proprietorship.

An LLC is an incorporated business organization that generally protects the owners from individual liability for the organization's obligations and against vicarious liability for the negligence and malfeasance of others. Management may be flexibly structured to allow owners (referred to as members) to apportion management authority as they see fit. Partnership classification is assured under some state statutes and may be attained through proper structuring in others.

Creating an LLC is as simple as forming a corporation. **Articles of Organization** must be filed with the Secretary of State; they are similar to the articles of incorporation used to form corporations. Filing fees are much the same.

An **operating agreement** defines the rights and obligations of the members, including how profits, losses and distributions will be shared. Most LLCs will have limitations on the transferability of members' interests and the ability of members to carry on the business after a member ceases to be involved.

Members are generally not liable for the debts and other obligations of the LLC, but they are liable for:

- The amounts the members have agreed to contribute to the LLC,

- Under some statutes, amounts distributed to the members, and

- Any negligence or malfeasance the member individually commits or that the member supervises.

This generally means that members are not liable for the contracts and general liabilities of the LLC or for any mistakes or improper actions of others in the name of the LLC.

One of the major advantages of an LLC is related to tax. If properly structured, it provides the benefit of one level of taxation; as with partnerships, any income generated by the company is passed through to the owners.

6. FISCAL YEAR-END

Four of the five entities that we have described in this chapter will, with rare exceptions, have a December 31st year-end.

The only one that can elect a different year-end is a regular corporation (C Corporation). The reasons for electing a non-calendar year-end might include:

- Matching the natural business cycle of the company,

- Delaying the payment of certain taxes, and

- Avoiding conflicts with vacations or particularly busy periods.

HOW WE CAN HELP

We'll be pleased to assist you with selecting a suitable legal entity and establishing your fiscal year-end.

CHAPTER 2

REGISTERING WITH THE TAX AUTHORITIES

By working faithfully eight hours a day you may eventually get to be boss and work twelve hours a day.

Robert Frost

CHAPTER 2

REGISTERING WITH THE TAX AUTHORITIES

As a business person you will quickly discover that you have extensive tax and information filing requirements with a number of different governmental agencies. Substantial penalties are routinely assessed if the required forms and returns are not properly prepared and filed on a timely basis. Several forms are required when starting a business. While this chapter is not intended to be an all-inclusive list of all filing requirements, it does summarize some of the more common ones. Consult with your legal and accounting professionals to make sure that you meet all the specific filing requirements of your business.

1.   INTERNAL REVENUE SERVICE

The Internal Revenue Service (IRS) is responsible for collecting Federal payroll taxes (including Social Security taxes, Federal unemployment taxes and Medicare taxes) and Federal Income taxes. All tax forms filed with the IRS require the use of a **Federal Employer Identification Number (FEIN)**. This number is obtained by filing a Form SS-4 by mail, fax or telephone. It can also be filed online at the IRS website, **www.irs.gov/smallbiz**.

File Form SS-4 early to obtain your FEIN *before* you are required to file tax returns. You can download Form SS-4 and instructions from www.irs.gov/formspubs/.

Payroll tax requirements are detailed in Chapter 3. Income tax filing requirements and tax planning are discussed in Chapter 4.

2. ILLINOIS DEPARTMENT OF EMPLOYMENT SECURITY

The Illinois Department of Employment Security (IDES) is responsible for collecting State Unemployment insurance contributions.

To obtain an IDES Account Number, you will need to file Form UI-1 with the IDES. You can download Form UI-1 with instructions from www.ides.illinois.gov.

With Illinois TaxNet you can file your monthly or quarterly wage report and pay via ACH Debit securely.

3. ILLINOIS DEPARTMENT OF REVENUE

The Illinois Department of Revenue (IDR) is responsible for collecting State Income Taxes.

You must file Form Reg-1 to register to do business in Illinois. You can download Form Reg-1 with instructions from www.revenue.state.il.us

You can file your monthly or quarterly reports online by registering for MyTax Illinois.

All forms filed with IDR require an identification number, which in the case of individuals is your social security number and in the case of other entities, your FEIN.

Successful Business Owners

1. Are totally dedicated to their customers
2. Know about customer loyalty & retention
3. Know their position in the market
4. Have a unique selling point that everyone knows about
5. Have a strategy to achieve this

4.   BUSINESS LICENSE

Some cities require a business license. You should inquire as to whether this is a requirement in the city in which your business is located. Applications can be obtained from City Hall or in some cases online. The fee for a Business License can range from $25 to $25,000, depending on the city and the size of the business. Your business license must generally be renewed annually.

HOW WE CAN HELP

Please call us and we'll help you register with the various tax authorities.

---

5.   TAX CALENDAR

Significant filing dates for a corporation using a calendar year-end are summarized as follows:

DATE	RETURNS
January 31st	Sales tax return* Payroll tax returns Annual Form W-2s issued to employees Form 1099s issued to payees
February 28th	Form W-2s filed with social security administration Form 1099s and 1096s filed with IRS
March 15th	Corporate income tax returns

January 31st	Payroll tax returns ACA Information Reporting Forms 1095-B and 1095-C due to employees Form 1099-MISC when reporting non-employee compensation payments in box 7 Form W-2, whether filed using paper forms or electronically
February 28th	Forms 1094-B, 1095-B, 1094-C, and 1095-C due to IRS if using paper form
March 15th	S-Corporation returns (Form 1120S) for corporations on a calendar year Partnership returns (Form 1065)
March 31st	Forms 1094-B, 1095-B, 1094-C, and 1095-C due to IRS if filing electronically
April 15th	Estimated income tax payments Individual income tax returns C-Corporation returns (Form 1120) for corporations on a calendar year Trust and Estate income tax returns Foreign Bank Account Reports (FinCen Form 114)
April 30th	Quarterly payroll tax returns
June 15th	Estimated income tax payments
July 31st	Quarterly payroll tax returns
September 15th	Estimated income tax payments Partnership returns on extension Corporate returns on extension

October 15th	Individual income tax returns on extension Foreign Bank Account Reports (FinCen Form 114)
October 31st	Quarterly payroll tax returns
November December	Year-end tax planning
January 15th	Estimated income tax payments

Note: Many of these requirements also apply to partnerships and sole proprietorships. When a year-end other than December 31st is used (see Chapter Five) some of these dates will vary.

When dealing in certain regulated industries, such as utilities or petroleum, there are also numerous other tax filing deadlines of importance.

* Larger companies may have to file sales tax returns on a monthly, quarterly or semi-annual basis.

FEDERAL AND STATE PAYROLL TAXES

Effective leadership is putting first things first.
Effective management is discipline, carrying it out.

Stephen Covey

CHAPTER 3

FEDERAL AND STATE PAYROLL TAXES

If you have employees, you will be responsible for collecting payroll taxes and filing payroll tax reports.

Failure to deposit payroll taxes in a timely manner results in substantial penalties and interest. New businesses frequently get into trouble because they do not follow the strict payroll tax rules. Be sure to consult your tax advisor ***before*** hiring employees. Decide who will be responsible for the payroll process, preparing the checks, depositing payroll taxes and preparing payroll reports. Because of the complexities involved, most businesses use a payroll service.

1. FEDERAL PAYROLL TAXES

The following chart contains tax rates and the taxable wage basis for employers and employees. Please contact our office for the most up to date information.

Social Security Tax (FICA) and Federal Unemployment Tax (FUTA)

	Medicare	Soc. Sec.	Total
FICA Tax rate for employer	1.45%	6.2%	7.65%
FICA Tax rate for employee	1.45%	6.2%	7.65%
On wages not to exceed	No Limit	$ 110,100	
Maximum employer contribution	No Limit	$ 8,170	
Federal Unemployment Tax (employer only): Gross Federal tax rate			6.0%
Less credit for Illinois Unemployment Insurance			5.4%
Net FUTA rate			0.6%
On Wages not to exceed			$7,000
Maximum employer contribution (per employee)			$56

In addition to the above Federal payroll taxes, you are required as an employer to withhold Federal income taxes from each employee according to the number of exemptions claimed.

2. FEDERAL PAYROLL TAX DEPOSIT REQUIREMENTS

The deposit requirements for employer *and* employee portions of Social Security Taxes (FICA) and Federal Income Tax Withheld (FIT) are as follows:

Lookback period. Your deposit schedule for a calendar year is determined from the total taxes reported on your Forms 941, in a four-quarter lookback period. The lookback period begins July 1 and ends June 30 of the prior year. If you reported $50,000 or less of taxes for the lookback period, you are a monthly schedule depositor; if you reported more than $50,000, you are a semiweekly schedule depositor.

New employers. During the first calendar year of business, the tax liability for each quarter in the lookback period is considered to be zero. Therefore, you are a monthly schedule depositor for the first calendar year of business. However, see the one-day depositor rule below.

1. **Monthly Depositor.** An employer that reported employment taxes of $50,000 or less during the lookback period generally must make only monthly deposits for the entire calendar year. The deposit for a month must be made on or before the 15th day of the following month.

2. **Semi-Weekly Wednesday/Friday Depositor**. An employer that reported employment taxes of more than $50,000 during the lookback period is a semi-weekly depositor for the entire year. Such employers must make deposits on or before Wednesdays or Fridays depending on the timing of their payrolls. Specifically, employment taxes from payments to employees made on Wednesdays, Thursdays or Fridays must be deposited on or before the following Wednesday. Taxes from Saturday, Sunday, Monday or Tuesday payments to employees must be deposited by the following Friday.

3. **Non-Banking Days.** Semi-weekly depositors have at least three banking days to make a deposit. If any of the three weekdays following the close of a semi-weekly period is a bank holiday, the employer will have an additional banking day to make the deposit. For example, if Monday is a bank holiday, deposits from the prior week Wednesday through Friday period can be made by following Thursday, rather than by the regular Wednesday deposit day.

4. **One-Day Depositor.** If a monthly or semi-weekly depositor accumulates employment taxes of $100,000 or more during a deposit period (monthly or semi-weekly), it must deposit the taxes by the next banking day. This rule overrides the normal rules for determining deposit dates discussed above. A monthly depositor that must make a one-day deposit under this rule immediately becomes a semi-weekly depositor **for the rest of the calendar year *and* the following year.**

---

5 Great Marketing Questions

Q. Why did we start this business?

Q. Where do our/will our first customers come from?

Q. Why do/will our customers buy from us?

Q. What is our single greatest advantage over the competition?

Q. What is our Unique Selling Proposition?

---

3. FEDERAL UNEMPLOYMENT TAXES

To determine your quarterly liability for FUTA, multiply by .008 that part of the first $7,000 of each employee's annual wages that you paid during the quarter. If the resultant liability for all employees for the quarter is $100 or less, there is no requirement to deposit it currently, you merely add it to your liability for the following quarter.

If your liability for any calendar quarter (plus any undeposited taxes for an earlier quarter) is more than $500, you are required to deposit the taxes by the end of the following month.

If the tax reported on your annual Federal Unemployment Tax Return, Form 940, less deposits for the year is:

1. **More than $500,** you must deposit by the last day of January.
2. **Less than $500,** you may pay the taxes when you file Form 940.

4. SUPPLEMENTAL WAGES

If supplemental wages – such as bonuses, commissions and over-time pay– are included in the same payment with regular wages, tax to be withheld is determined as if the total of the supplemental and regular wages were a single payment for the regular payroll period.

If supplemental wages are not paid with the same payment as the regular wages, the employer may:

1. Withhold at a flat rate of 25% for Federal.

2. Combine the supplemental wage with the last regular wage, determine the tax on the total wage, and then subtract the amounts already withheld on the regular wage payment.

5. FRINGE BENEFITS

Gross income does not include fringe benefits that qualify for exclusion, as described in the categories listed below. Fringe benefits that qualify for the exclusion are exempt from Income Tax and Social Security tax withholding. Conversely, benefits that do **not** qualify are subject to these taxes. An example of a common non-qualifying benefit subject to tax is the automobile allowance.

No-additional-cost service. Some services to an employee are excludable if (1) they are offered for sale to the public in the ordinary course of the employer's line of business in which the employee works, and (2) the employer does not incur substantial additional cost. For example, employers who furnish airline travel or hotel rooms to employees working in these lines of businesses in such ways that non-employee customers are not displaced and employers incur no substantial additional cost can exclude the cost of the room or travel from the employee's gross income.

Qualified employee discount. Any employee discount is an excludable qualified employee discount if: (1) in the case of property, it does not exceed the gross profit percentage of the price at which the property is being offered to customers; (2) in the case of a service, it does not exceed 20% of the price at which the service is being offered.

Working condition fringe. Any employer-provided property or services are excludable benefits to the extent that they are deductible as ordinary and necessary business expense had the employee paid for them. Under certain conditions, the fair market value of a qualified demonstration automobile used by a full time auto salesperson is an excludable working condition fringe.

De minimus fringe. Property or services not otherwise tax-free are excludable if their value is so small as to make accounting unreasonable or administratively impractical. An operation of any eating facility for employees is an excludable de minimus fringe if it is located on or near the employer's business premises and the revenue derived normally equals or exceeds the direct operating costs of the facility.

Qualified Moving Expenses Reimbursement. An employee may exclude from gross income an amount received from an employer for payment of qualified moving expenses.

Transportation Fringe Benefits. An employee may exclude from gross income certain maximum amounts received from an employer as reimbursements for transit passes, vanpooling expenses and qualified parking expenses.

6. OTHER TAX REQUIREMENTS

Whenever a wage payment is made, the employer must provide the employee with a statement of gross wages and specific deductions (if any). You use the Form W-4 submitted by the employee and the tax tables provided in the employer's tax guides to determine the correct income tax to withhold. If the employee fails to submit a Form W-4, the employer must withhold at the rate applicable to a single person who has no withholding exemptions. Employers must submit, with their quarterly payroll tax returns, a copy of any Form W-4 on which an employee is claiming the equivalent of 10 or more withholding exemptions.

An employer must also complete a Form I-9 for each employee and obtain the necessary documentation to verify eligibility status.

When making a reimbursement or payment of moving expenses to an employee, the employer must complete and furnish the employee with a Form 4782.

An employer must furnish a Form W-2 to each employee showing remuneration and withheld taxes for each calendar year. Flat rate expense account allowance, disability insurance paid by the employer and moving expense reimbursements are among the items to be included as other compensation on a Form W-2. Upon request, a Form W-2 must be furnished to a terminated employee within 30 days after the request or the final wage payment, whichever is later. All other Forms W-2 should be given to the employees by January 31st of the following year.

7. AVAILABLE PUBLICATIONS

Circular E, Publication 15, Employer's Tax Guide, which covers the payroll tax reporting and deposit requirements, is available at the local office of the Internal Revenue Service or on the IRS website, www.irs.gov. Search the website by using the key word "Publication 15."

8. ILLINOIS PAYROLL TAXES

The Illinois Department of Employment Security regulates the state unemployment tax. The taxable wage base and rate for employers changes each year based on the employer's experience rate (history of unemployment use by former employees) and annual state changes. The limits and maximum contributions are per employee. Please contact our office for the most up to date rates.

In addition to the above payroll taxes, you are required as an employer to withhold State Personal Income taxes (SIT) from each employee according to the number of exemptions claimed. This is remitted to the Illinois Department of Revenue.

9. ILLINOIS PAYROLL TAX DEPOSIT REQUIREMENTS

Due dates for deposits of SIT are based on an employer's *federal* payroll tax deposit schedule/requirement.

Illinois Quarterly Filer -Form IL-941 Quarterly Wage and Withholding Report is due the last day of April, July, October and January of the following year. Monthly deposits are required by the 15th of each month if you are a quarterly filer. You may be assigned to make payments semi-weekly depending on when you pay your employees and the schedule assigned to you. If you are assigned to the semi-weekly payment schedule you must make your withholding payment electronically.

Illinois Annual Filer -Form you are assigned as an annual filer your annual return is due January 31st of the following year. Do not file annually unless you have been notified by the Department to do so. You will not qualify to be an annual filer if your withholding exceeds $12,000 during a quarter. Your payments are still due on a monthly basis even if you are an annual filer.

EFT transactions for Quarterly payments must settle into the State's bank account on or before the next business day following the last timely date for the quarter.

Monthly deposits are due by the 15th of the following month.

EFT transactions for Monthly deposits must settle into the State's bank account on or before the next business day following the due date.

You may also want to review the Illinois Department of Revenue website at www.revenue.state.il.us or the Illinois Department of Employment Security website at www.ides.illinois.gov. See Publication 131 for additional information.

10. EMPLOYEE VS. INDEPENDENT CONTRACTOR

A major area of uncertainty and potential dispute relates to whether a worker is classified as an employee or as an independent contractor. All else being equal, it is much less costly to the employer if a worker is an independent contractor — avoiding social security and other payroll taxes. However, if someone is subsequently reclassified by the authorities as an employee, the penalties can be substantial. This can happen, for example, when a terminated "independent contractor" files for unemployment benefits and claims to have really been an employee.

The IRS has developed a twenty-factor control test to help determine whether the person providing the service should be classified as an employee or an independent contractor. Illinois has three addition tests – see below.

20 FACTORS

ELEMENTS	EMPLOYEE	INDEPENDENT CONTRACTOR
1. Instructions	Employee is required to comply with instructions about when and where work is done.	An independent contractor decides how to do the job, establishes his/her own procedures, and is not supervised.
2. Training	Employee may be trained by other experienced employee working with him or her, by correspondence, by required attendance, or by other methods.	An independent contractor uses his/her own methods and receives no training from the principal.
3. Integration	If the worker's services are so integrated into an employer's operations that the success or continuation of the business depends on the performance of the services, it generally indicates employment.	An individual's performance of service & those of assistants affect his or her own business reputation.
4. Services rendered personally	If the services must be rendered personally, it indicates the employer is interested in the methods as well as results.	A contractor having right to substitute another's services without the principal's knowledge suggests the existence of an independent relationship.

ELEMENTS	EMPLOYEE	INDEPENDENT CONTRACTOR
5. Hiring, Supervising, paying assistants	If a worker hires or supervises an assistant at the employer's direction, he/she is acting as a representative of the employer.	An independent contractor hires, supervises and pays assistants under a contract with him/her.
6. Continuing relationship	The existence of a continuing relationship between a worker and the person whom he/she performs services indicates an employee status.	The relationship between an independent contractor and his/her client ends when the job is finished.
7. Set hours of work	Employer sets hours of work for the worker.	An independent contractor is the master of his/her own time.
8. Full time work	Full time work for the business is indicative of control by employer. Full time does not necessarily mean an eight-hour day or five-day week but may vary with the intent of the parties and nature of occupation.	An independent contractor is free to work whenever he/she chooses.

ELEMENTS	EMPLOYEE	INDEPENDENT CONTRACTOR
9. Work done on premises	An employee works on the employer's premises or on the location designated by employer.	An independent contractor can work away from the principal's premises.
10. Order or sequence of work	An employee performs services in order or sequence set by employer.	An independent contractor is free to perform services to complete the work as he/she prefers.
11. Reports	A submission of regular oral or written reports indicate control since the worker must account for his/her actions.	An independent contractor is not required to file the reports that constitute a review of his/her work.
12. Payments by hour, week, month	Payment by hour, week, month indicated employee status.	Payment to contractors is usually by a flat fee for the job or by working hours.
13. Payment for worker's business and traveling expenses	Payment by employer indicates control over worker.	Are paid on a job basis and the contractor takes care of all incidental expenses.
14. Tools and Materials	Tools and materials are normally furnished by employer.	An independent contractor furnishes his/her own tools, and materials.

ELEMENTS	EMPLOYEE	INDEPENDENT CONTRACTOR
15. The extent of the worker's investment	All necessary facilities are furnished by employer.	An independent contractor often (but not necessarily) has a significant investment status in the facilities he/she uses in performing services.
16. Profit and Loss	When workers are insulated from loss or restricted in the amount of profit gained, they are usually employees.	The possibility of a profit or loss for the worker as a result of his/her services shows independent contractor status who invests significant amounts of time or capital in his/her work without any guarantee of success.
17. Works for more than one person or firm	A worker may work for a number of people or firms and still be an employee of one or all of them because he/she works under control of each firm.	An independent contractor works for a number of persons or firms at the same time. He/she can work freely, not controlled by any firms.
18. Offers services to the general public	If a worker performs services alone, does not advertise his/her services to general public, does not hold licenses or hire assistants, and performs services on a continuing basis, it	An independent contractor is free to seek out business opportunities, advertise, maintain a visible business location, and is available in the general public.

ELEMENTS	EMPLOYEE	INDEPENDENT CONTRACTOR
	is an indication of an employment relationship.	
19. Right to discharge	If the employer has the right to discharge a worker at will and without liability, the worker is considered an employee.	An independent contractor cannot be discharged as long as he/she produces a result that measures up to his/her contract specification; relationship can be terminated with liability.
20. Right to quit	The right to quit at any time without incurring liability indicates an employer-employee relationship.	If an individual agrees to complete a specific job and he/she is responsible for its satisfactory completion, it indicates the independent contractor status.

For more information refer to IRS publication 15-A, Employer's Supplemental Tax Guide, and talk with us.

11. ILLINOIS INDEPENDENT CONTRACTOR

The Department of Employment Security has a simple 3-point test to help determine whether the person providing the service should be classified as an employee or an independent contractor. Services performed by an individual shall be deemed to be employment unless and until any of the following are proven.

1. Such individual has been and will continue to be free from control or direction over the performance of such services, both under his contract of service and in fact; AND
2. Such service is either outside the usual course of business for which such service is performed or that such service is performed outside of all the places of business of the enterprise for which such service is performed; AND
3. Such individual is engaged in an independently established trade, occupation, profession, or business.

12. FORM 1099 FILING REQUIREMENTS FOR INDEPENDENT CONTRACTORS

There are annual reporting requirements for payments to independent contractors. Payments are reported on form 1099 MISC –In general, you are required to file a form 1099 if you have paid a person at least $600 in rents, services (including parts and materials). You must have the name and address and SSN or FEIN for each payee. You can obtain this information during the year by requiring the person to complete a form W-3 when you engage them for their services.

It is extremely important to report the 1099 payment information correctly. The government agencies use this information to determine if the payee has included the income on their tax return.

You may want to review the instructions for Form 1099 at irs.gov. There are several exceptions to filing form 1099.

HOW WE CAN HELP

Please call us and we will be pleased to help get you set up for payroll and payroll taxes and various reporting requirements.

CHAPTER 4

INCOME TAXES

In this world nothing can be said to be certain,

except death and taxes.

Benjamin Franklin

CHAPTER 4

INCOME TAXES

Income tax laws are extensive, complicated and constantly changing. While this chapter is not intended to cover all ramifications of income taxes, it does provide some general guidelines for complying with the main income tax rules.

1. INCOME TAX REPORTING

Each type of legal entity is required to file a different type of income tax form, as follows:

1. Sole Proprietorship: A sole proprietorship is considered a component of the individual's personal tax return. Schedule C, the required tax form, is included with the owner's Form 1040 and for Illinois Form 1040. If the business has net taxable income, then Schedule SE must be prepared to determine the amount of self-employment tax that is due to the Federal Government (this is the self-employed equivalent of social security taxes).

Successful Business Owners
✓ Work smarter NOT harder
✓ Measure accurately how they're doing
✓ Forecast ahead and monitor progress
✓ Control costs with budgets
✓ Have a financial strategy

2. Partnership: A partnership is not a taxable entity. It is treated as a conduit through which taxable income is passed to the individual partners for inclusion in their respective tax returns. The partnership is required to file Federal Form 1065. For Illinois a Form 1065 is required. No income tax is due with these forms, however, included with the forms is a Schedule K-1, which lists the various items of income and credits to be included on the individual partners' returns.

3. C Corporation: A C Corporation is considered a taxable entity and is required to file a Federal Form 1120 and Illinois Form 1120.

4. S Corporation: An S Corporation is a type of corporation that has special treatment under the tax laws. Generally, this type of entity is treated in the same manner as a partnership, with certain exceptions. Tax forms required are Federal Form 1120S and Illinois Form 1120S.

5. Limited Liability Company: A limited liability company and its cousin, a limited liability partnership (used typically by professional service providers) are generally not taxable entities and are treated as a conduit though which taxable income is passed to the individual partners or members for inclusion in their respective tax returns. These entities are generally required to file the same forms as a partnership, Form 1065. No income tax is due with the forms, however, included with the forms is a Schedule K-1, which lists the various items of income and credits to be included on the returns of the individual partners or members.

2. ESTIMATED TAX PAYMENTS

In addition to the regular tax forms, the law specifies that if an estimate of the tax is not properly prepaid on a quarterly basis, a non-deductible underpayment penalty is to be levied. Since an estimate is based on forecasting the future, and liable to human error, the tax laws provide two safe-harbors to avoid the penalty for underpayment. If your payments for each quarter equal the lesser of 100% of the prior year's tax or 90% of the current year's tax, then the penalty can be avoided. In some cases you may have to pay 110% of the prior year Federal tax liability to avoid the penalty.

There are exceptions to the underpayment penalty, one of which is the annualized income installment method. Required quarterly payments can be calculated based on actual income and deductions in each quarter. If income was higher in later quarters of the year, this method may reduce the penalty by lowering required quarterly payments at the beginning of the year.

Estimates can be made online or are filed using the following forms:

Corporate	Federal tax deposit Form 8109 deposited with your bank.
	Illinois Form IL-1120-ES.
Individual	Federal Form 1040-ES.
	Illinois Form IL-1040-ES.

3. DUE DATES

Due dates of the various forms are:

1. Sole Proprietorship:	Federal Form 1040 and Illinois Form IL-1040 are due on April 15th. Estimated tax payment Forms (Federal Form 1040-ES and Illinois Form IL-1040-ES) are due quarterly on April 15th, June 15th, September 15th and January 15th.
2. Partnership:	Federal Form 1065 and Illinois Form IL-1065 are due the 15th day of the 3rd month after the end of the tax year - March 15th for almost all partnerships.
3. C Corporation:	Federal Form 1120 and Illinois Form IL-1120 are due the 15th day of the 4th month after the end of the tax year. Federal & Illinois tax deposits are due the 15th day of the 4th, 6th, 9th and 12th month of the tax year.
4. S Corporation:	Federal Form 1120S and Illinois Form IL-1120S are due the 15th day of the 3rd month after the end of the tax year.

| 5. *Limited Liability Company:* | An LLC may be treated as a partnership *or* corporation for tax purposes. The due dates will follow the classification (see above). |

4. EXTENSIONS

Businesses and individuals may request an extension of time to file tax returns. However, these extensions <u>do not extend the time for paying the tax.</u>

5. FIRST TAX RETURN

The first tax return of a business is very important. Elections are made which will dictate the way the business is taxed for many years to come.

Some of the more significant elections that will need consideration are outlined below:

1. Election to capitalize and amortize costs incurred to organize the business. These can be legal, accounting or similar fees paid to commence operations. Such costs are not normally considered expenses of the corporation and are not deductible unless this election is made.

2. Election to accrue vacation pay earned but not taken by employees at the end of the tax year. Without this election, vacation pay is not deductible until the year it is taken.

3. Accounting method used to report for tax purposes:

   - Cash
   - Accrual
   - Other hybrid method

4. Method of inventory valuation.

5. Method of accounting for long term contracts.

The elections discussed above are only a few of those that may need to be considered in an initial return. It is important to plan how best to utilize elections to take advantage of some of the following provisions of the Federal and Illinois tax laws including:

- Net operating loss carryovers.
- Research and development tax credits.
- Business energy tax credits.
- Illinois tax credits.

6. STATE TAXES

If your company conducts, or plans to conduct, business in more than one state, it is essential that you familiarize yourself with the applicable tax laws and filing requirements for each state. If you are not in compliance, you may be prohibited from doing business in those states. You may also subject yourself to significant penalties and interest.

HOW WE CAN HELP

Taxes are our "bread and butter" — the laws are very complicated, so we recommend that you retain us to prepare your income tax returns. Any amount you might save by doing your own returns can be more than offset by the costs of making mistakes.

A bigger issue than making mistakes is missing the significant tax savings opportunities available to businesses, particularly on an initial return.

Proper tax planning is also essential to realize the greatest benefit from the income tax laws. This is a year-round process requiring communication on both sides — you and us. Please let us help you in this important area.

CHAPTER 5

ACCOUNTING AND BOOKKEEPING

You have to know accounting. It's the language of practical business life. It was a very useful thing to deliver to civilization. I've heard it came to civilization through Venice which of course was once the great commercial power in the Mediterranean. However, double entry bookkeeping was a hell of an invention.

Charlie Munger, Vice Chairman Berkshire-Hathaway

CHAPTER 5

ACCOUNTING AND BOOKKEEPING

As an owner of a business, it is vitally important that you have the financial information you need to run the business effectively. You will also need financial information to provide to outsiders such as the bank and to the taxing authorities.

The necessity for good, well-organized financial records cannot be over emphasized. One of the mistakes made by some entrepreneurs is not keeping good financial records and therefore not having sufficient information to make good business decisions or not receiving warning signals of potential problems such as a likely future cash crunch.

Good, timely financial reports do not necessarily require complicated bookkeeping or accounting systems. An appropriate system is like any tool used in your business; it needs to be sophisticated enough to provide the information you need but simple enough that you or your assistant or bookkeeper can run it.

Questions you will want to ask in developing your accounting and financial reporting system are:

1. Who will need and want to see the financial information?

2. What information do we need to manage the business?

3. What information will be needed to satisfy the government, regulatory and taxing authorities?

Please seek our assistance in developing a system that will consistently provide the right information on a timely basis.

1. THE ACCOUNTING PROCESS

Accounting is the process of collecting, organizing, maintaining, and reporting financial information. Let's review the process:

Everything starts with the creation of source documents which record your business transactions. Source documents include:

- Sales invoices
- Cash receipts
- Cash register tapes
- Purchase invoices
- Checks
- Miscellaneous, such as petty cash items

5 Key Performance Indicators (KPIs) for Every Business

✓ Revenue
✓ Gross Profit %
✓ Accounts Receivable Days
✓ Average Transaction Value
✓ Overhead as a % of Revenue

<u>Journals</u>. Journals (also known as "books of original entry") are where the information from the source documents are recorded in a prescribed way.

- Sales are recorded in a <u>Sales Journal</u>
- Purchases are recorded in a <u>Purchase Journal</u>
- Cash receipts are recorded in a <u>Cash Receipts Journal</u>
- Checks are recorded in a <u>Cash Disbursements Journal</u>

<u>General Ledger</u>. Once all the source documents have been recorded in the journals, the summary totals are transferred to a general ledger, where the balances of each account are displayed. A listing of these account balances is known as a "trial balance".

What we have described to this point is generally referred to as "bookkeeping" or "write-up work". At the end of a time period — usually a month — we want to summarize everything that has been done during the period and create reports, known as "financial statements".

Adjusting Entries. But before we can generate the financial statements, we need to carefully review what's been done and make sure that "what the books say" reflects reality. Part of this activity involves reconciliations of the bank accounts, receivables and payables.

We then make various adjusting entries to record such items as:

- depreciation
- payroll taxes
- bad debts, and
- bank charges

The next step is to prepare Financial Statements.

2. FINANCIAL STATEMENTS

A basic set of financial statements consists of a balance sheet, a profit and loss statement and a statement of cash flow.

Balance Sheet. Your balance sheet reports the financial position of your company as of a given date. Think of it as a "snapshot" of the business. Your balance sheet has 3 elements: assets, liabilities, and equity. Assets are things you own. Examples include:

- Cash
- Accounts receivable
- Inventory
- Equipment
- Furniture and fixtures
- Deposits (such as rent deposits)

Liabilities are what you owe. Examples include:

- Accounts payable
- Notes payable
- Payroll taxes payable

- Accrued interest payable

Equity is the difference between what you own and what you owe, i.e. what's your worth. The equity section of the balance sheet is in turn broken down into subsections tracking how much the owner(s) contributed to the business, how much the business has made (or lost) and how much the owner(s) took out.

Profit and Loss Statement. Your profit and loss statement (also called an "income statement" but most frequently referred to as a "P & L") shows the profit or loss of the business during a specific period of time. The elements of a P & L are:

- Income (or Revenue)
- Cost of Goods Sold
- Operating Expenses
- Net Profit (or net income)

Operating expenses are usually grouped into categories, for example, as follows:

- Labor and personnel
- Marketing expenses
- Occupancy expenses
- Office expenses
- General and administrative
- Other

Design your own groupings to give yourself the information you need to run the business.

Cash Flow Statement. Your cash flow statement shows you the changes in your cash position over a period of time — where it came from and where it went. The cash flow statement is broken down into 3 major categories:

1. Cash Flows from Operating Activities — This represents the cash flow generated from the business, which will be different from the net profit because of changes in receivables, inventory,

accounts payable and fixed assets. (For example, buying inventory does not affect your P & L until you sell it, but it does affect cash.)

2. Cash Flows From Investing Activities — This represents the cash flow movement from buying or selling assets held for investment and similar activity.

3. Cash Flows From Financing Activities — This represents the cash flow movement from borrowing or repaying money and receiving or paying back money put in by the owner(s).

The Cash Flow Statement helps you reconcile the age-old dilemma, "if we made all this money, why don't we have any cash?"

3. RESPONSIBILITY FOR BOOKKEEPING AND ACCOUNTING

Bookkeeping and accounting are such important functions that it makes sense early on to assign clear responsibilities for their regular, consistent execution.

Important questions for you to ask are:

1. Who will keep the books of the business?

2. Will your receptionist or assistant double as a part-time bookkeeper?

3. Will you have an outside bookkeeper that comes in periodically, or will the volume of activity require a full-time bookkeeper?

Business owners often decide to keep the books themselves, and underestimate the time commitment required. Other demands of the business (such as making sales!) may create a time crunch resulting in record keeping receiving a low priority. Keeping the books requires regular allocation of time. Close control can be achieved by personally signing checks and scrutinizing key documents and records, such as the monthly bank statement.

> CONTROL TIP: Have all bank statements sent to your home address, so that you can perform a quick review before passing them to someone else to reconcile.

Let's revisit the steps in the bookkeeping and accounting process:

Source Documents. These are prepared by the business as part of normal day-to-day operations.

Journals. These are usually prepared in-house using an automated accounting program such as QuickBooks.

General Ledger. The general ledger is generally created as a by-product of the above steps when using a program like QuickBooks.

Trial Balance. This is in effect a print-out of the general ledger.

Adjusting Entries. Some of the adjusting entries can be made in-house, particularly on interim month-end closings. At year-end, we, as your CPAs, would make needed year-end adjusting entries.

Financial Statements. Interim financial statements can be prepared in-house depending on the level of expertise available. Year-end financial statements would normally be part of our responsibility or a coordinated effort.

As CPAs, we are available to assist in the bookkeeping and accounting function depending on your needs and availability of time and personnel. For example, if you only want to produce the source documents, we can complete all the other steps. At the other end of the spectrum, you may be able to complete all the steps and just have us help with finalizing the year-end financial statements and tax returns.

4. CASH OR ACCRUAL ACCOUNTING

One of the decisions to be made early on is whether to keep your books on a cash or accrual basis.

The cash basis of accounting has the advantage of simplicity. Income is recorded when money is received and expenses are recorded when money is paid out.

The **accrual basis** is a much better reflection of what is actually happening in your business. It matches the revenue generated in a particular time period with the costs and expenses of generating that revenue, even if the related cash receipts or disbursements take place in some other time periods. Income is recorded when you earn it (e.g. make a sale) and expenses are recorded when you incur them. Keeping books on an accrual basis is more time-consuming but the information generated is worth the effort.

Whether you use the cash or accrual basis, it is often possible to report for tax purposes on a different more advantageous basis. We can advise you on possibilities in your particular circumstances.

5. INTERNAL CONTROL

Internal control is a system of checks and balances designed to ensure that company assets are properly safeguarded, and that the financial information produced is accurate and reliable. If you are personally handling all of the company's financial transactions, maintaining good internal control is relatively straight forward.

However, when a company grows to the size that delegating some functions becomes necessary, it is more difficult to ensure that all transactions are being accounted for properly. As soon as you delegate tasks and functions, there are potential internal control issues.

No matter the size of your business, you want to be able to answer "yes" to the following questions:

1. When we provide goods or services to our customers, can we be certain that sales are always properly recorded and the cash is collected?

2. When we pay out cash, can we be certain that we received the proper goods or services?

There are a number of steps to establishing good internal controls, the principal one being: do not let anyone control a financial function from start to finish. That way, for fraud to take place, you would have to have collusion.

Examples of internal control steps:

- The individual preparing sales invoices should be different from the person recording them.

- The person preparing and recording checks should not be allowed to sign them. And it's a good idea to require dual signatures on checks if it's practical.

- The person receiving the bank statement should not be the same person who reconciles the bank. As suggested already, have bank statements sent to your home address.

Example Fraud Checklist

Fraud is a potential threat to every company. Review the checklist below and if you answered No to any questions, an internal controls review might be a worthwhile exercise.

	Yes	No

1. Do you have a code of conduct that explicitly prohibits employees from committing fraud, having conflicts of interest or engaging in any other form of illegal or unethical behavior?
    a. Have all your employees, vendors and customers received a copy of it?
    b. Have key employees provide annual confirmation of their compliance?		

2. Do you have a clear company policy on time and expense reporting?		
3. Do you verify the credentials (including bank details) of all new vendors before they are authorized to supply your company?		
4. Do you make sure all disbursements are properly approved?		
5. Do you use direct deposit for payroll?		
6. Do you require two signatures on checks over a certain amount?		
7. Do you review the bank statements before anyone else does? You might want to consider having them sent to your home address.		
8. Do you review cancelled checks (or copies) and match payee names with endorsements?		
9. Do you review invoices for any payees you don't recognize?		
10. Do you make sure bank statements are reconciled each month and that your CPA reviews the bookkeeper's work periodically?		
11. Do you make sure everyone takes their full allotted vacation time?		
12. If something seems odd, whether it is a disbursement to an unfamiliar vendor or an unexpected expense, do you have a system in place to verify the information?		

SAMPLE ONLY – THIS CHECKLIST IS GENERAL BUSINESS ADVICE AND SHOULD NOT BE CONSTRUED AS SPECIFIC TO YOUR SITUATION. PLEASE CONSULT THE APPROPRIATE ADVISORS.

6. COMPUTER SYSTEMS

Since the development of double-entry bookkeeping (first documented by an Italian monk, Luca Pacioli in 1495), the advent of the computer has had the simple greatest impact on accounting.

Virtually every business in America has a computer system of some kind, generally running some kind of accounting package. There are several packages available and they are quite affordable, robust and easy to learn. The most popular is QuickBooks, but there are several others. We have experience with a variety of accounting software packages that can help you run your business more efficiently. It is important to choose software that will best meet your particular needs.

HOW WE CAN HELP

We are available to assist you with:
- Setting up a proper accounting system
- Helping you identify your key performance indicators (KPIs) and develop a measuring and monitoring system
- Establishing appropriate internal controls
- Selecting a computerized accounting package, setting up the system and providing training

---

CHAPTER 6

CASH MANAGEMENT

Profit in business comes from repeat customers, customers that boast about your project or service, and that bring friends with them.

W. Edwards Deming

CHAPTER 6

CASH MANAGEMENT

CASH IS KING! The lifeblood of any business is its ability to collect cash. We often encounter small businesses that are profitable yet don't generate enough free cash to pay the day-to-day expenses and the owners.

Being able to anticipate cash resources is an important part of running a successful enterprise.

1. STARTING THE ANALYSIS

The starting point for forecasting your cash flow is the volume of sales you expect to generate. Your sales forecast must be as finely tuned as possible.

Some factors to consider in your sales forecast include:

- Expected market share
- Sales history
- Competitive analysis
- Product lines
- Number and quality of sales people or distributors
- Seasonality
- Local economic conditions
- Time horizon

2. CASH COLLECTIONS

Once you have completed your sales forecast, you now need to calculate how sales will convert to cash. So you will need to estimate:

- What percentage of sales are paid in cash?
- What percentage are credit sales where you have to carry accounts receivable?
- What percentage are credit card sales where processing fees will be deducted?
- What percentage of the credit sales do you expect to collect in:
    - 30 days?
    - 90 days?
    - More than 90 days?
- What percentage might we never collect (bad debts)?
- What discounts are you planning to offer for prompt payment?
- How much of our collections are for sales tax which will need to be remitted to the taxing authority?
- What other sources of cash are planned (such as rents from subtenants, loans, or owner investment)?

Once you are comfortable with the timing of the collections of funds from sales and other sources, it's time to look at the costs, expenses and other cash outflows of your business.

3. CASH OUTFLOWS

As you start to work on the outflow or disbursement side of your forecast, you will want to consider the following questions related to cost of sales:

- If your business requires inventory, do you purchase the merchandise from others or do you purchase component parts and assemble them?

- What are the credit terms your vendors are willing to offer? Do you have to pay for purchases on a COD basis or can you get credit for thirty, forty-five or even 60 days?
- What costs are required to convert purchased items into salable merchandise?

- What supplies are needed to be kept on hand to pack and ship merchandise?

- How many employees will you need and at what cost?

- How much machinery will be required and at what cost?

Once you have addressed the cost of sales issues, including the costs of carrying inventory and processing it, it's time to consider all the other expenses of operating the business.

If we take all the ongoing monthly expenses as a given, let's look at some other expenditures that you may face in the first year of business. Here's a partial checklist:

- First and last month's rent
- Rent security deposit
- Purchase of furniture, or deposit if a rental
- Purchase of fixtures and equipment
- Purchase of computers, peripherals and installation costs
- Utility deposits
- Organization costs (if you're a corporation)
- Lawyer's fees for drafting agreements, incorporating your business and reviewing your lease agreement
- Accountant's fees for setting up the accounting system and establishing the Chart of Accounts
- Tenant improvements
- Business licenses
- Stationery
- Signs
- Logo design fees
- Initial inventory of supplies

- Loan repayments

When you're preparing your forecast, it may seem like the list of costs and expenses is endless. However, it is imperative to make the list as detailed as possible to ensure that you have sufficient funds to make your operation viable and to avoid running out of cash. Remember, one of the primary causes of small business failure is under capitalization

In addition to determining cash outlays you will have to make, it is critical to determine the timing of such payments. A good rule of thumb for cash flow planning is to assume that you are going to have to pay your expenses sooner than you think and that you will collect your cash slower than you anticipate. If you use this approach, any negative surprises should be minimal.

Preparing cash flow projections can be time consuming and tedious. We can help! We have software programs that can do most of the "heavy lifting" and where you can do "what if" analysis and get an immediate answer. Your personal involvement in the process is, of course, critical because these are your projections, not ours, and only you know what it takes to run the business.

The more effort **you** put into developing the cash flow projections, the more accurate and useful they will be. You may also discover potential savings that you had not previously considered.

HOW WE CAN HELP
We are here to assist you with strategic planning, cash management, profit improvement and benchmarking — these are all services designed to help your business reach its full potential.

FINANCING YOUR BUSINESS

Sometimes when you innovate, you make mistakes. It is best to admit them quickly, and get on with improving your other innovations.

Steve Jobs

CHAPTER 7

FINANCING YOUR BUSINESS

Financing is the engine of commerce and in this chapter, we will address the issue of obtaining credit and financing your business. Most businesses will have an access financing at some point along the way.

You may need capital for the initial outlays prior to opening your business or you may require funds for expansion or for additional working capital during seasonal peaks. Generally, business financing can take two forms: debt or equity.

Debt means borrowing money. Loans for start-up businesses usually come from one or more of these sources:

- Vendor or Trade Credit
- Personal credit cards
- Family
- Friends
- Banks
- Small Business Administration (SBA) guarantees
- Leasing companies
- Customers or clients
- Specialist lenders
- Investors

Equity involves giving up an ownership interest in exchange for money or other assets. This can take many forms, depending on which kind of legal entity you have selected.

If you have a partnership, you might sell a regular partnership interest. If you have a limited partnership (such as an LLC), you might sell a limited partnership interest.

If you have a corporation, you can issue common stock, preferred stock, stock options or warrants, or a combination. This is a complex area and subject to very strict federal and state regulations designed to protect investors. Get your attorney involved <u>before</u> you start discussions with potential investors.

The 4 Ways to Grow Your Business

1. Increase your prices.
2. Increase your number of customers and how often they do business with you.
3. Increase the amount your customers spend with you each transaction.
4. Decrease your expenses.

1. FINANCING ALTERNATIVES

As we have just outlined, there are a number of different types of debt and equity financing. Financing may even be a combination of debt *and* equity tailored to fit your company's requirements.

Let's look at the different sources of financing in more detail.

2. DEBT FINANCING SOURCES

<u>Vendor or Trade Credit</u>. An important source of financing for small companies is credit from vendors and suppliers. Many suppliers will initially ask for cash on delivery (COD) or a prepayment before starting on your order. Most suppliers will offer you credit terms once you have gained their confidence by continuing to do business with them and paying on time. Establishing good relationships with vendors is essential, because if you buy on credit, you can often resell the purchased goods or services to your customers before you have to pay for them.

Many vendors will rely on your trade credit history as you establish additional vendor relationships. Trade credit terms vary depending on the type of purchase you make, the industry you are buying from, and the industry you are in. It makes sense to contact a number of vendors and even to pay a higher price for goods and services in exchange for more liberal payment terms.

Personal Credit Cards. An astonishing number of small businesses actually; use personal credit cards as a major source of financing. In fact, prior to going into business, many people apply for new credit cards just to have some credit available to them. The downside, of course, is that credit cards often have a very high rate of interest, particularly after they pass the low-interest "tease"" period. Also having too many credit cards can negatively affect your credit rating.

Family and Friends. Many businesses are launched with help from family and friends who are more likely to be flexible on repayment terms.

Banks. Banks typically lend to small businesses on a secured basis using equipment, inventory, or accounts receivable. The more liquid and readily salable the assets you can offer as collateral, the more acceptable they are likely to be to a banker. Loans from a bank may take several forms, such as:

- A line of credit that allows you to borrow up to a predetermined maximum as you need it and pay it back as funds from operations become available.

- A note payable in full on an agreed date.

- An installment loan for the purchase of a specific asset such as a computer or office furniture.

- A longer-term fully-amortized loan over 3-5 years.

Unless you have a long-established credit history and a strong balance sheet, the bank will require personal guarantees from the principals.

Small Business Administration (SBA) Guarantees. The SBA, an Agency of the Federal Government, has a program whereby it will guarantee up to 90% of a loan to a small business. Most banks participate in this program. The SBA can also guarantee mortgages if you are buying your premises or guarantee leases if you are leasing.

Leasing Companies. In today's business environment it is common to acquire equipment through a lease agreement. Leasing companies are willing to take a higher degree of risk than banks and accordingly their funding is more expensive than commercial bank loans.

Leases typically run for 3 to 5 years with monthly lease payments — and then at the end of the lease, there is a pay-off amount, either pre-agreed or fair market value, which allows you to get ownership of the asset. The effective interest rate is not stated in the lease agreement (since it's technically not a loan) but we can calculate it for you to make sure that leasing is the appropriate decision.

Customers or Clients. Often, the impetus for going into business is a favorite customer or client who says, "you should go out on your own," and who promises to do business with you. Asking for a modest loan is a good way to test their sincerity and finance your business. It also guarantees they are going to patronize the business!

Specialist Lenders.   There are specialist lenders that specialize in financing a particular type of acquisition (such as a medical practice) or a particular type of asset (such as a printing press).

Investors. Investors may structure all or part of their investment as a loan, as this will give them greater security. Such a loan will likely be convertible into equity, at the investor's option.

3. EQUITY FINANCING SOURCES

Equity financing means selling a portion of your business. You may have already decided to take in partners in exchange for an investment or you have family or friends who have invested in exchange for equity.

If these are not available or do not yield sufficient capital, there are professional investors to consider.

Venture capital companies.   A venture capital company is in the business of taking risks. It is usually backed by a group of investors who may be individuals or corporations. The investors are represented by a management group that evaluates potential investments and manages the existing investments.

The cost of venture capital financing is high compared to other forms of financing but that's because venture capitalists are dealing with high risk situations that most lenders wouldn't contemplate, and there are usually no viable alternatives.

A venture capital firm will expect to get back at least 3-7 times its investment over a 5 year period. The venture capital firm can provide depth of experience and management assistance in areas where your management team may be weak. It can also provide valuable contacts and introductions. The cost of venture capital is measured in terms of the portion of your company you must give up in order to obtain the level of investment you need.

Private individuals. Sometimes successful individuals who have accumulated substantial wealth get into the business (or hobby) of investing in start-ups and other small companies. They are referred to as "business angels".

The business acumen and contacts of these individuals can be a valuable asset to your business. An individual investor can react to an opportunity more quickly than a venture capital firm and can be more flexible in the type of investment structure used.

4. HOW DO I GET THE MONEY?

Regardless of the type of financing you're looking for, the process of obtaining it is the same. Develop a Business Plan that addresses these 5 basic questions:

1.   What is your business proposition and how will you make it successful?

2.   Do you have the necessary experience and have you done your homework?

3. How much money do you need?

4. How will you spend the money?

5. How will you pay it back?

The business plan usually covers a 3 to 5 year period and includes financial forecasts. Financial forecasts are like weather forecasts-the farther out you go, the less reliable they become.

Here's a typical table of contents for a business plan:

1. Executive summary (including a statement of purpose and policy)
2. Background
3. Details of the product or service
4. Details of management and personnel
5. Details of other assets and resources
6. Marketing information
7. Financial information
8. Projected profit and loss statements
9. Timeframes

HOW WE CAN HELP

Because we have been in practice in this community for a long time, we know most of the bankers and other funding sources. We are pleased to make introductions as appropriate.

We can also assist you in developing your business plan.

CHAPTER 8

INSURANCE

*There is only one boss. The customer. And he can
fire everybody in the company from the chairman
on down, simply by spending his money
somewhere else.*

Sam Walton

CHAPTER 8

INSURANCE

Insurance is not the favorite outlay for new businesses — one more place where money goes out and nothing comes in. That is, until something goes wrong. Then it's a great investment.

There are many different insurance policies available to businesses. Your accountant and insurance agent can help you review the amounts and kinds of coverage required to insure against both the general and specific risks that could have a significant impact on your business. The terms of your building or office lease or mortgage may require certain kinds of insurance coverage in specified minimum amounts. If you have leased equipment or have borrowed money from a bank or other lender there will likely be insurance requirements in those agreements.

Insurance companies typically offer package policies which can be customized to provide comprehensive coverage of your unique needs. Make sure that your insurance policies are thoroughly reviewed each year — things change.

1. POLICIES

Here are some insurance policies that may be required or appropriate to your business:

1. **Workers' Compensation Insurance.** Workers' compensation insurance coverage is required by law. Employees are covered for on the job injuries, as well as vehicle coverage. Your insurance agent can explain the details of required coverage, rating systems and assist with policy purchase.

2. **Health Insurance.** Health insurance is the principal benefit offered by employers and the most sought after by employees. Much has changed recently with the enactment of the Patient Protection and Affordable Care Act which is intended to provide

a minimum level of coverage to most individuals. It requires most US citizens and legal residents to carry health insurance — some people will be eligible for tax credits to help pay for coverage and those opting not to buy will be subject to penalties.

The new Act does not require you as an employer to offer health insurance but it does incentivize you in 2 ways:

1. Each state will set up an "exchange" where small businesses can pool their risks, which presumably will save money.

2. A Small Employer Health Insurance Tax Credit is available with a tax credit of up to 35% of an employer's contributions.

3. **Property and Casualty Insurance.** This covers you against the loss of property by fire, theft, etc. Equipment should be insured for its replacement value.

    If a new lathe costs $10,000, that is what it must be insured for. What the lathe is worth second-hand or what it's recorded at on your books is irrelevant. If you lose your lathe, the proceeds will be needed to buy you a new one. The replacement value of equipment is often much higher than you think. Insurance of leased equipment will also generally be your responsibility.

4. **Vehicle Insurance.** All vehicles have to be insured - at least for public liability.

Tip: To make sure you don't have a catastrophic loss of data in the event of loss or destruction of your computer systems, consider using an on-line backup service.

---

5. **Product Liability.** This covers you in case any products that you manufacture or supply cause injury or damage to a third party or their property.

6. **Professional Liability Insurance.** This type of insurance (also known as malpractice insurance) is common to professionals and is often mandated for certain professions such as accounting and law to cover claims from clients for negligent acts, errors or omissions. Other professionals such as management consultants or IT consultants are advised to investigate this type of coverage.

> **Key Credit Policy Questions**
> 1. Are all new customers asked for suitable credit references?
> 2. Are credit references checked?
> 3. Are credit limits set, reviewed and adhered to?
> 4. What is the system to handle delinquent receivables?

7. **Life Insurance.** Your own life should be insured so that your family is protected from economic hardship in the event of your demise. The amount of coverage needed will depend on several factors including the number of your dependents, their ages or what other assets you have. Whole life insurance may be appropriate if you can afford it; otherwise term insurance provides needed coverage at a modest cost.

8. **Disability Insurance.** Make sure you consider disability insurance to protect against the possibility of a long-term disability or illness. A person in their 40s is 15 times more likely to be unable to work because of illness or disability than from death.

9. **Keyperson Insurance.** Keyperson insurance allows a business to insure the life or health of any employee whose death or prolonged absence would cause the business to suffer. It is ordinary life or health insurance, but with the business as the beneficiary.

10. **Business Interruption**: Covers the loss of revenue should your business be forced to shut down due to reasons beyond your control, such as flood, fire or earthquake.

11. **Legal Fees.** Insurance is generally available to businesses to cover your legal fees should you be involved in a lawsuit.

12. **Employee Fidelity Bond.** This covers the risk of loss from theft or dishonesty by employees. If your business deals in large amounts of cash, negotiable securities, or similar types of assets, you are well advised to consider this coverage. In fact, it is appropriate for any business where an employee has potential access to assets of the business, customers or clients. Certain businesses are required to carry this type of insurance.

13. **Umbrella Coverage.** This covers losses over and above the limits of your other policies. Umbrella policies are especially valuable if you, or your business, have a net worth requiring protection in the event of a catastrophic loss.

14. **Buyout Insurance.** Your business may have a requirement for the remaining shareholders or partners to buy out the interest of a shareholder or partner who dies. This can be covered by buyout insurance.

There are many other types of policies and reasons to consider them. Check with a qualified insurance broker who specializes in dealing with businesses.

Insurance is like any other product you purchase. Do your homework. Before you buy, get lots of input about your needs and options.

HOW WE CAN HELP
Call us and we'll be pleased to recommend a qualified insurance broker.

SELECTING PROFESSIONAL ADVISORS

You can't operate a company by fear, because the way to eliminate fear is to avoid criticism. And the way to avoid criticism is to do nothing.

Steve Ross

CHAPTER 9

SELECTING PROFESSIONAL ADVISORS

Building a successful business involves developing alliances and a network of trusted advisors.

We're here to help. We will be pleased to provide services in the areas where we specialize.

These include:

- Income tax preparation
- Tax planning
- Accounting
- Bookkeeping
- Auditing
- Payroll and Sales Taxes
- Wealth Management
- Financial Planning
- Strategic Planning
- Profit improvement
- Benchmarking
- Key Performance Indicator monitoring

We are also pleased to introduce you to other professionals such as:

- Attorneys
- Bankers
- Insurance Brokers
- Real Estate Agents
- Printers
- I.T. Consultants
- Payroll Services
- Financial Advisors
- Pension Consultants

FEDERAL FORMS

All forms can be downloaded from www.irs.gov/formspubs/

Form SS-4	Instructions
Form SS-4	Application for Employer Identification Number
Form W-4	Employee's Withholding Allowance Certificate
Form I-9	Employment Eligibility Verification
Form W-2	Wage and Tax Statement
Form W-3	Transmittal of Wage and Tax Statements
Form W-9	Request for Taxpayer Identification Number and Certification
Form 1096	Annual Summary and Transmittal of U.S. Information Returns
Form 1099-MISC	Miscellaneous Income
Form 941	Employer's Quarterly Federal Tax Return
Form 940	Employer's Annual Federal Unemployment (FUTA) Tax Return

ILLINOIS FORMS

The following forms can be downloaded from
www.revenue.state.il.us/TaxForms.

Form Reg-1   Illinois Business Registration Application

Form IL-941   Quarterly Wage Report

The following forms can be downloaded from www.ides.illinois.gov

Form UI-1   Report to Determine Liability
Form UI-3/40   Employer's Contribution and Wage Report

www.ingramcontent.com/pod-product-compliance
Lightning Source LLC
Chambersburg PA
CBHW080601180526
45168CB00007B/2739